MW00681065

A Special Gift

For:

Anna

From:

The Bush Family

Date:

March 2000

Copyright © 1997
Brownlow Publishing Company
6309 Airport Freeway
Fort Worth, Texas 76117

All rights reserved.
The use or reprinting of any part of this book without the express written permission of the publisher is prohibited.

ISBN, 1-57051-168-3

Design: Koechel Peterson & Associates

Printed in Singapore

Quiet Moments
Of Inspiration

Little Treasures Miniature Books

A Child's Tea Party
A Little Cup of Tea
A Little Nest of Pleasant Thoughts
All Things Great & Small
All Things Grow With Love
Angels of Friendship
Baby's First Little Book
Baby's First Little Book of Angels
Beside Still Waters

Dear Teacher

Faithful Friends

For My Secret Pal

From Friend to Friend

Grandmothers Are for Loving

Mother—The Heart of the Home

My Sister, My Friend

Precious Are the Promises

Quiet Moments of Inspiration

Quilted Hearts

Rose Petals

Soft As the Voice of an Angel

The Night the Angels Sang

'Tis Christmas Once Again

True silence is the rest of the mind
and is to the spirit what sleep is to the body,
nourishment and refreshment.

WILLIAM PENN

God takes life's pieces and gives us unbroken peace.

W. D. GOUGH

A faithful friend is a strong defense; and he that
hath found such a one hath found a treasure.

JOSEPH ADDISON

The Power of Listening

Listening is a magnetic and strange thing, a creative force. The friends who listen to us are the ones we move toward, and we want to sit in their radius. When we are listened to, it creates us, makes us unfold and expand.

KARL MENNINGER

Quieted by His Love

The Lord your God is with you,
he is mighty to save.
He will take great delight in you,
he will quiet you with his love,
he will rejoice over you with singing.

ZEPHANIAH 3:17

Everything true
and great grows
in silence.
Without silence
we fall short
of reality and
cannot plumb the
depths of being.

LADISLAUS BOROS

Wise are they who can take the little moment as it comes and make it brighter ere 'tis gone.

SHAKER PROVERB

Such as are thy habitual thoughts, such also will be the character of the mind. For the soul is dyed by the thoughts.

MARCUS AURELIUS

It takes a long time to become young.

PABLO PICASSO

Normal day, let me be aware of the treasure you are. Let me learn from you, love you, savor you, bless you before you depart. Let me not pass you by in quest of some rare and perfect tomorrow. Let me hold you while I may for it will not always be so. One day I shall dig my nails into the earth, or bury my face in the pillow, or stretch myself taut, or raise my hands to the sky, and want, more than all the world, your return.

MARY JEAN IRION

A true friendship is as wise as it is tender. The parties to it yield implicitly to the guidance of their love, and know no other law nor kindness.

HENRY DAVID THOREAU

Quiet Beauty

Your beauty should be that
of your inner self, the unfading
beauty of a gentle and quiet spirit.

1 Peter 3:3, 4

Friendship

Friendship is the comfort of
knowing there is always a shoulder to
lean on, a hand to reach out for,
and a heart to welcome me home.

ANONYMOUS

An inexhaustible good nature is one of the most precious gifts of heaven, spreading itself like oil over the troubled sea of thought, and keeping the mind smooth and equable in the roughest weather.

WASHINGTON IRVING

Only connect!
Live in fragments no longer.

E. M. FORSTER

Any concern too small to be turned into a prayer is too small to be made into a burden.

CORRIE TEN BOOM

To like and dislike the same things,
that is indeed true friendship.

SALLUST

Quiet Minds

Quiet minds can not be perplexed or frightened, but go on in fortune or misfortune at their own private pace, like a clock during a thunderstorm.

ROBERT LOUIS STEVENSON

He who is filled with love is filled with God himself.

AUGUSTINE

The main reason for healing is love.

PARACELSUS

What sweet delight a quiet life affords.

WILLIAM HAWTHORDEN DRUMMOND

Life Within

Our true life lies at a great depth within us. Our restlessness and weaknesses are in reality merely strivings on the surface.

EMANUEL SWEDENBORG

Dews of Quietness

Drop thy still dews of quietness,
Till all our strivings cease;
Take from our souls the strain and stress,
And let our ordered lives confess
The beauty of thy peace.

JOHN GREENLEAF WHITTIER

We blossom under praise like flowers
in sun and dew; we open, we reach, we grow.

GERHARD E. FROST

Make it your ambition to lead a quiet life,
to mind your own business and to
work with your hands.

1 THESSALONIANS 4:11

All Is Well

I want, by understanding myself,
to understand others. I want to be all that
I am capable of becoming. This all sounds
very strenuous and serious. But now that
I have wrestled with it, it's no longer so.
I feel happy—deep down all is well.

KATHERINE MANSFIELD

Everything has its wonders,
even darkness and silence.

HELEN ADAMS KELLER

Familiar acts are beautiful through love.

PERCY BYSSHE SHELLEY

It is in silence that God is known,
and through mysteries that he
declares himself.

ROBERT H. BENSON

After silence,
that which comes nearest
to expressing the
inexpressible is music.

ALDOUS HUXLEY

My Task

To love some one more dearly every day,
To help a wandering child to find his way,
To ponder o'er a noble thought and pray.
And smile when evening falls—
this is my task.

Maude Louise Ray

HOW SWEET the words of truth breathed from the lips of love.

JAMES BEATTIE

A smile of encouragement at the right moment may act like sunlight on a closed up flower, it may be the turning point for a struggling life.

ANONYMOUS

The Sunlight of Silence

Every man who delights in a multitude
of words, even though he says admirable things,
is empty within. If you love truth,
be a lover of silence. Silence, like the sunlight,
will illuminate you in God and will deliver
you from the phantoms of ignorance.
Silence will unite you to God himself.

ISAAC OF NINEVEH

Minutes of Gold

Two or three minutes—two or three hours,
What do they mean in this life of ours?
Not very much if but counted as time,
But minutes of gold and hours sublime,
If only we'll use them once in a while
To make someone happy—make someone smile.
A minute may dry a little lad's tears,
An hour sweep aside trouble of years.
Minutes of my time may bring to an end
Hopelessness somewhere, and bring me a friend.

AUTHOR UNKNOWN

To analyze the charms of flowers
is like dissecting music; it is one of those
things which it is far better to enjoy than
to attempt fully to understand.

TUCKERMAN

It is always good to know, if only in passing,
a charming human being; it refreshes our
lives like flowers and woods and clear brooks.

GEORGE ELIOT

Love is a choice—not simply,
or necessarily, a rational choice,
but rather a willingness to be present
to others without pretense or guile.

CARTER HEYWARD

Strength of character may be acquired
at work, but beauty of character is learned at
home. There the affections are trained. There
the gentle life reaches us, the true heaven life.

HENRY DRUMMOND

Live peaceful and quiet lives in
all godliness and holiness.

1 TIMOTHY 2:2

And remember, we all stumble,
every one of us. That's why it's a comfort
to go hand in hand.

EMILY KIMBROUGH

Listening to the Silence

But now I have learned to listen
to silence. To hear its choirs singing the
song of ages, chanting the hymns of space,
and disclosing the secrets of eternity.

KAHLIL GIBRAN

God is a tranquil being and abides in a tranquil eternity. So must your spirit become a tranquil and clear little pool, wherein the serene light of God can be mirrored.

GERHARD TERSTEEGEN

Waiting in Silence

You need not do anything
Remain sitting at your table and listen
Just wait
And you need not even wait,
just become quiet and still and solitary
And the world will offer itself to you to be
unmasked
It has no choice
It will roll in ecstasy at your feet.

RAINER MARIA RILKE

The great acts of love are done
by those who are habitually performing
small acts of kindness.

ANONYMOUS

Cherish all your happy moments: they
make a fine cushion for old age.

CHRISTOPHER MORLEY

The two words "peace" and "tranquility" are worth a thousand pieces of gold.

CHINESE PROVERB

Happiness is neither within us; nor without us; it is the union of ourselves with God.

BLAISE PASCAL

Love is the only force capable of transforming an enemy into a friend.

MARTIN LUTHER KING, JR.

The greatest
ideas, the
most profound
thoughts,
and the most
beautiful poetry
are born from
the womb
of silence.
William Arthur Ward

Who among us has
not sought peace in a song?

VICTOR HUGO

Look for strength in people,
not weakness; for good, not evil.
Most of us find what we search for.

J. WILBUR CHAPMAN

Bring thy soul and interchange with mine.

JOHANN FRIEDRICH VON SCHILLER

The capacity to care
gives life its deepest significance.

PABLO CASALS

Yesterday is history, tomorrow is a mystery,
and today is a gift;
that's why they call it the present.

ANONYMOUS

The more one loves the
nearer he approaches God,
for God is the spirit of infinite love.

R. W. TRINE

Nothing is more simple than greatness;
indeed, to be simple is to be great.

RALPH WALDO EMERSON

A Sweet Friendship

It is a sweet thing, friendship, a dear balm,
A happy and auspicious bird of calm,
A flower which, fresh as Lapland's roses are,
Lifts its bold head into the world's pure air,
And blooms most radiantly when others die.

PERCY BYSSHE SHELLEY

Have patience with all things,
but chiefly have patience with yourself.
Do not lose courage in considering your
own imperfections, but instantly
set about remedying them—
every day beginning the task anew.

St. Francis de Sales

They are never alone who are accompanied with noble thoughts.

PHILIP SIDNEY

Every part is disposed to unite with the whole, that it may thereby escape from its incompleteness.

LEONARDO DA VINCI

Not one thing which you have ever done for God has been lost; not one is lost or ever will be lost.

EDWARD BOUBERIE PUSEY

A Faithful Friend

A truly faithful friend is the medicine of life;
a truly faithful friend, a strong covering.
For what would not a genuine friend do?
What pleasure would he not create for us?
What profit? What safety? Though thou
were to name a thousand treasures, there is
nothing comparable to a real friend.

ARETHUSA TO ST. JOHN

If you give
your life as a
wholehearted
response to love,
then love will
wholeheartedly
respond to you.
MARIANNE WILLIAMSON

Gentle Words

What the dew is to the flower,
Gentle words are to the soul,
And a blessing to the giver,
And so dear to the receiver,
We should never withhold.
Gentle words, kindly spoken,
Often soothe the troubled mind,
While links of love are broken
By words that are unkind.
Then O, thou gentle spirit,
my constant Guardian be,
"Do to others," be my motto,
"as I'd have them do to me."

POLLY RUPE

In quietness and in confidence shall be your strength.

ISAIAH 30:15

The man who has no inner life is a slave to his surroundings.

HENRI FRÉDÉRIC AMIEL

No love, no friendship can cross the path of our destiny without leaving some mark on it forever.

FRANÇOIS MAURIAC

Where I was born and where and how I have lived is unimportant. It is what I have done with where I have been that should be of interest.

GEORGIA O'KEEFFE

When the
heart overflows
with gratitude,
or with any
other sweet
and sacred
sentiment,
what is the
word to which
it would give
utterance?
A friend.

W. S. LANDOR

Illustration Credits

Brownlow Private Collection:
Page 53

Fine Art Images, Inc.:
Pages 3, 10, 23, 26, 47, 48, 58, 61, cover

Fine Art Photographic Library, Ltd.:
Pages 7, 15, 19, 29, 31, 34, 36-37,
40, 43, 57, 62-63

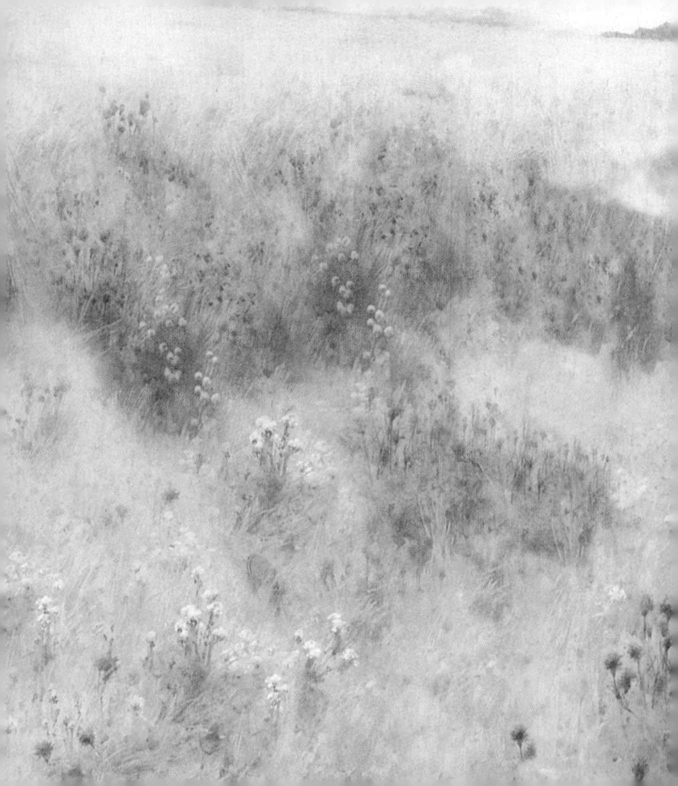